WINGS OF THE MORNING

TO JUNE
who made this book possible

WINGS OF THE MORNING

Frank Topping

Illustrated by Cetra Long

LUTTERWORTH PRESS
Cambridge

Lutterworth Press
7 All Saints' Passage
Cambridge CB2 3LS

By the same author: ***Lord of the Evening***
Lord of my Days
Lord of Life
Lord of the Morning
Working at Prayer
The Words of Christ
Lord of Time

British Library Cataloguing in Publication Data
Topping, Frank
    Wings of the morning.
    I. Title
    821'.919   PR6070.05/
    ISBN 0-7188-2675-2

Printed in Great Britain by The Guernsey Press Co. Ltd., Guernsey, Channel
Islands.

CONTENTS

Meditations on the Letter of St Paul to the Romans

MEDITATIONS
ON
THE PSALMS

MINDFUL OF ME

'O Lord, our Lord,
how majestic is your name
in all the earth.
When I look at the heavens,
the work of your fingers,
the moon and the stars
which you have established,
what is man that you are mindful of him?
Who am I, that you are mindful of me?

— Psalm 8.1, 3-4

I remember, as a child,
lying in bed,
closing my eyes and thinking,
'Who am I? Why am I me?
Does God really know *me?*'.
In time the child grew
and learned
about anger, envy,
ambition, money, people,
war, suffering and love.
And the child, now a man, concluded
that the only important thing
was to matter to someone,
to be wanted, to belong,
or, simply, to love and be loved.
And the question became
not, 'Does God know *me?*'
but, 'Do I know him?',
for if love is the only thing
worth living for,
then God is love.

'When I look at the heavens,
the work of your fingers,
the moon and the stars
which you have established,
what is man that you are mindful of him?'

If the mind of God is love,
if the purpose of God is love,
if God is love,
then teach me, Lord, to be mindful of you.

I SHALL NOT WANT

'The Lord is my shepherd,
I shall not want;
he makes me lie down
in green pastures.
He leads me beside still waters;
he restores my soul.'

— Psalm 23.1-3

Lord,
I am always in want
of stillness and comfort;
Good shepherd,
restore my soul.

There is hardly a day
when I am not mulling over
my needs, my wants.
I convince myself
that I know what I need
to make things right,
to improve my lot.
I find it hard to trust
in the promise
that 'I shall not want',
so I grit my teeth and struggle on,
finding neither rest nor stillness,
until, in desperation, I cry out,
'Lord, restore my soul.'
And it is then,
in spite of my headstrong stupidity,
that the shepherd
reveals the still waters
of his love.

It is then that I can rest
in him.
It is then
that I can lie down
in peace.

'The Lord is my shepherd,
I shall not want;
He makes me lie down
in green pastures.
He leads me beside still waters;
he restores my soul.'
Lord,
help me to put my trust in you,
the shepherd of my life.

I WILL NOT FEAR

'Even though I walk
through the valley of the shadow of death,
I will fear no evil,
for thou art with me;
thy rod and thy staff
they comfort me.'

– Psalm 23.4

Lord,
how well I know these words,
but how little do I live by them.
I fear the shadows
and forget
that you are with me.

Only in your strength am I able
to face adversity with fortitude,
illness with courage,
death with faith
and sorrow with hope.
Remind me,
when all seems lost,
that nothing can overcome your love.
Your rod is my strength,
your staff, my hope.
And if my anxieties
cannot be removed
in faith, give me knowledge
of the love
that will enable me to face
the worst that can happen,
with courage, even joy.
For you are the God

of yesterday and tomorrow,
of death and life everlasting.

Lord,
in faith,
'Even though I walk
through the valley of the shadow of death,
I will fear no evil,
for thou art with me;
thy rod and staff
they comfort me.'

AN OASIS OF CALM

'Thou preparest a table before me
in the presence of my enemies;
thou anointest my head with oil,
my cup overflows.
Surely goodness and mercy shall follow me
all the days of my life;
and I shall dwell in the house of the Lord
for ever.'

— Psalm 23.5-6

In the presence of my enemies
I am not alone,
even when I am surrounded
by things going wrong.
Within me
is all the power I need,
an oasis of calm,
an unassailable fortress,
the knowledge of the love of God
which can make even my soul
a temple of the Holy Spirit.
Lord,
I am not worthy of your love,
yet you offer
more than I can comprehend.
My cup does indeed overflow.
In your generosity
of goodness and mercy
may I defeat the enemies
within me.

May I quieten bitterness with understanding,
conquer fear with trust
and quell anger with love.

'Thou preparest a table before me
in the presence of my enemies,
thou anointest my head with oil,
my cup overflows.
Surely goodness and mercy shall follow me
all the days of my life;
and I shall dwell in the house of the Lord
for ever.'

LOVE NEEDS NO WORDS

'I will guard my ways
that I may not sin with my tongue,
I will bridle my mouth
in the presence of the wicked.'

— Psalm 39.1

And just so
the suffering servant, Isaiah,
did not open his mouth,
and Jesus, before his accusers,
was silent.

Goodness does not argue,
it speaks for itself.

In country after country,
in year after year,
revolutionaries shake their fists
and shout for freedom.
Barrels of ink
pour from the pens of philosophers.
Politicians pose on platforms
making points with accusing fingers.
But the man in the tin-roofed hospital
is quiet when he tends the sick,
and the girl in the desert,
where the hungry wait,
is too busy to talk,
and the nuns are praying silently
in the presence of the dying.

Lord, forgive me
that I talk much
and do little.

Help me to see
that mercy does not take sides,
generosity needs no persuasion,
goodness no argument,
and love no words.

'I will guard my ways
that I may not sin with my tongue,
I will bridle my mouth
in the presence of the wicked.'

And the suffering servant, Isaiah,
did not open his mouth,
and Jesus, before his accusers
was silent.

Goodness does not argue,
it speaks for itself.

A NEW SONG

'I waited patiently for the Lord;
he inclined unto me
and heard my cry.
He drew me up from the desolate pit,
out of the miry bog,
and set my feet upon a rock,
making my steps secure.
He put a new song in my mouth,
a song of praise to our God.'

– Psalm 40.1-3

How many crises,
problems, dilemmas
have clouded my horizon?
How many hopes and dreams
have faded?
How many
shattering blows,
betrayals,
doors slammed in my face?
Yet how many doors have opened?
How many fresh starts,
new beginnings
have been made?
The essence of nature
is death and rebirth,
perhaps the essence of God
is death and rebirth,
and the purpose of God's love
is to draw us
through darkness into light.

Perhaps eternity
is an infinite number
of new beginnings.
There is no gap
between the end of night
and a new day's dawn.
Yet each day is a new creation,
a new composition,
a new song.

Lord,
daily you lift me
from darkness to light,
you offer forgiveness and renewal,
you offer me life.
In the hours ahead,
let me see resurrection
in every meeting,
feel love
in every conversation,
feel hope
in every action.
O Lord,
put a new song in my mouth,
a song of love,
of life,
of praise.

HELP UNFAILING

'I lift up my eyes to the hills.
From whence does my help come?'

— Psalm 121.1

Lord,
I lift up my eyes
and see my own anxiety,
the worry that intrudes
no matter how I try to shut it out,
that haunts my day
and frets my sleep.
Lord,
from where does my help come?

This is not my first crisis,
nor will it be the last.
Time and again
I have met goblins of worry,
seen giant waves
rise up to engulf me.
Yet still
I have not been overwhelmed.
Hopes and fears,
dreams and disasters
litter my wake,
yet still I am here,
looking up once more to you.
For you are the one constant,
unchanging strength of my life.

When friends desert me,
you remain.
When my body fails,
you support me.
When my thoughts are in turmoil,
you bring peace.

'From whence does my help come?
My help comes from the Lord
who neither slumbers, nor sleeps,
the Lord who made heaven and earth.'

'The Lord will keep you from all evil;
he will keep your life.
The Lord will keep
your going out and your coming in
from this time forth and for ever more.'

FORGIVING AND FORGIVENESS

'Out of the depths I call to you,
Lord, hear my cry for help.
Listen compassionately to my pleading.
If you never overlooked our sins
who could survive?'   — Psalm 130.1-3

Lord, in this new day
help me to survive,
to start again.

Your forgiveness wipes my slate clean.
Your love blots out all my sins
as if they had never happened.
Your forgiveness is like rebirth,
a chance to start again
with a new, fresh life.
I have only to ask
and your forgiveness is immediate.
Lord,
teach me to forgive
as I am forgiven.
There are so many spoiled friendships,
so many marred relationships.
Sons, daughters,
brothers, sisters,
wives and husbands,
all aching for reconciliation,
for a chance to start again.

Teach me your life-giving generosity;
no matter who is right
or who is wrong,
help me to sweep away the bitterness,
the nurtured anger,
the stored up resentment of years.
Enable me, enable us, to start again.

'Out of the depths I call to you,
Lord, hear my cry for help.
Listen compassionately to my pleading.
If you never overlooked our sins
who could survive?'

Lord,
this day
help me to survive,
to forgive and be forgiven.
Help me to start again.

KNOWING ME

'O Lord, thou hast searched me
and known me.
Thou knowest when I sit down
thou discernest my thoughts from afar.
Thou searchest out my path and my lying down,
and art acquainted with all my ways.
Even before a word is on my tongue
though knowest it altogether.'

– Psalm 139.1-4

The mother thinks she knows her child,
the teacher hopes to understand the pupil,
the man to know himself.
But in all of us there are hidden depths,
hidden sometimes from ourselves.
Only when alone,
in prayer,
is light shone
in the corners we conceal.
Lord,
do not let me hide
behind pretence,
do not let me deceive myself.
Reveal the complex disguises
I have invented
to convince myself
that I am loving, generous,
honest, open.

Give me the courage
to see not only what I am
but what I was meant to be,
a child of God,
growing into the stature of your love.

'O Lord, thou hast searched me
and known me.
Thou knowest when I sit down
and when I rise up;
thou discernest my thoughts from afar.
Thou searchest out my path and my lying down,
and art acquainted with all my ways.
Even before a word is on my tongue
thou knowest it altogether.'

WINGS OF THE MORNING

'Whither shall I go from your spirit?
Or whither shall I fly from your presence?
If I ascend to heaven thou art there!
If I make my bed in Sheol, thou art there!
If I take the wings of the morning
and dwell in the uttermost parts of the sea,
even there thy hand shall lead me,
and thy right hand shall hold me.'

– Psalm 139.7-10

Why have I so often tried
to hide from God,
or rather, tried to dismiss
the presence of God?
When things are going well,
I think I do not need God,
so I forget him,
for weeks, months or longer.
The job, the career, the house
fill my mind, until, for a while
God becomes a mere childish memory,
needed only by the weak-minded.
Then suddenly, he is before me,
in beauty or in tragedy,
at all the points that matter,
in birth and death,
in pain, hunger and joy.
I see him in an act of love so perfect,
in a sacrificial life so moving
that I am shaken from my humanistic reverie.

And the shallow days
of my self-centredness
are seen for what they are,
fleeting, wispy, lost days
dispersed by the breath of God.

'If I ascend to heaven, thou art there!
If I make my bed in Sheol, thou art there!
If I take the wings of the morning
and dwell in the uttermost parts of the sea,
even there thy hand shall lead me
and thy right hand shall hold me.'

Lord,
help me to be aware of your presence
not only at the extremities of my life
but in every waking hour.

MEDITATIONS
ON THE
GOSPEL OF ST JOHN

BEGINNING WITH LIGHT

'In the beginning was the Word'

— John 1.1

In the beginning was the word,
in the beginning was — reason,
in the beginning was — the mind,
and the mind was with God,
and the mind was God,
and the mind of God dwelt among us
and became the light that was the light of men;
and the light shines in the darkness,
and darkness cannot quench light.

Darkness, in its rage, has taken up arms,
and the weapons of darkness
are envy, greed and fear;
its agents are suspicion, mockery and malice;
its battleground is the mind of man;
its bitter successes are divisions and conflicts
in homes and nations.
Its triumphs are poverty, hatred, violence and death.
But the greatest darkness
is always defeated
by the smallest light.
Light which makes dreams possible,
which brings hope to the downhearted,
comfort to the weary,
healing to the sick,
peace to troubled minds;
and the victories of light
are joy and love and life.

Lord,
you who are the light of men,
fill me with light,
lighten my path
that I might not stumble.
Shine on the complex shadows
of my pride, passions and self-interest
that they may fade
in the brightness of love.
Throughout the hours of this day
when anger and dissension cloud the horizon
may I see the light of reconciliation;
in the gloom of doubt
may there be sparks of hope,
and may your wisdom, peace and joy
be the light which lightens every day.

LIFE IN THE SPIRIT

'God is spirit
and those who would worship him
must worship in spirit and truth.'

– John 4.24

There does not seem to be much room
for spirituality
in the average day.
Most days are filled
with the practical and the material,
food, clothes, travel,
shopping, filling up with petrol,
answering letters, filling in forms,
answering the phone, catching the bus,
seeing the doctor, the dentist,
and watching television;
there does not seem to be much time
for exploring the spiritual dimensions
of being alive.

But the life of the spirit
is not restricted to holy places,
worship and spirituality
is not confined to churches,
chapels and monasteries.
The spirit lives
in people.
There is spirituality in a smile,
in generous words,
in an act of kindness,
in courtesy.

There is spirituality in patience and understanding.
Everything we do, and say, and think,
no matter how mundane and ordinary,
can be transformed by the spirit.

God is spirit
and we should worship
in spirit and truth,
To worship in truth
is to do the truth,
hope the truth,
love the truth,
live in truth.
Lord, in this moment
fill my heart and mind
with the knowledge of your presence,
that whatever I do this day
may be guided by your spirit and truth.
'Lord, thou knowest that I shall be busy this day,
if I forget thee, do not thou forget me.'

CASTING STONES

'Let him who is without sin
cast the first stone.'

– John 8.7

When men, filled with anger
and indignation,
pointed accusing fingers at a sinner
they considered worthy of stoning
and asked Jesus for a judgement,
Jesus said,
'Let him who is without sin
cast the first stone.'

Day after day,
in the newspapers and on television and radio,
critics, commentators and politicians
stand on their dignity
and point accusing fingers.
On trains and buses,
in homes, offices and works' canteens,
people like me are tempted
to shake the head
and make judgements about friends and colleagues.
But all of us would be silenced
if we were to hear Jesus saying,
'Let him who is without sin
cast the first stone.'

Jesus does not condone sin,
but he demonstrates
the quality of mercy,
the mercy of God towards sinners.

Jesus may hate the sin,
but he loves the sinner
and his love is revealed in mercy.
Perhaps my judgements would not be so harsh,
nor my accusations so quick,
if I were able to put myself in the position
of the person being judged,
remind myself of my own mistakes,
my own weaknesses,
my very secret failures.

God, preserve me from self-righteousness,
prevent me from being mentally pompous.
In your mercy is forgiveness
and the opportunity to start again
in the difficult business
of being a human being.
Give me generosity of mind and spirit.
Let me examine my own conscience
before I judge others.
Let me possess that quality of mercy
which neither condemns nor condones
but heals and restores.
Throughout the conversations of this day,
when judgements are made,
let me hear your voice saying,
'Let him who is without sin
cast the first stone.'

THE LIGHT OF LIFE

'I am the light of the world,
he who follows me will not walk in darkness,
but will have the light of life.'

– John 8.12

Light has many qualities.
After a storm, how welcome the sunlight;
everything feels more cheerful
when the sun is shining.
Even mean streets and shabby houses
look better, feel better, in sunlight.
How welcome the freshness and light
of spring
after the gloom of a long winter;
and even winter days can be lifted
by the cold bright light of a winter sun.
But strong light
can also reveal the cobwebs,
the dust and dirt
that lie more comfortably
in the dark.

The light of Christ,
the light of love,
is sometimes too bright for comfort.
In the light of love
greed and self-interest are revealed.
Conspirators prefer the shadows.
Jealousy and suspicion take root
and grow strong in the dark.

And the light that came into the world, in Christ,
was too uncomfortable, too disturbing;
and in dark places men plotted
to put out that light,
only to learn that the light of love
can never be extinguished.

Lord,
despite my fear
of what your light will reveal
in the dark corners of my soul,
let the light of your love
shine on me.
May my daily life,
my work, my conversation,
be bright with the light of love.
Wherever people plan for the future,
in politics and governments,
may they see that peace and prosperity
can be enjoyed only
when men and women begin to see
that love
is the light of the world.

BUT NOW I SEE

'One thing I know,
I was blind, but now I see.'

– John 9.25

Blind from birth
yet given sight by Christ —
they asked the man,
'Was Jesus good or a sinner?'.
He could not answer,
he did not know, but, he said,
'One thing I know,
I was blind, but now I see.'

And still the nature of Christ is questioned,
and people argue about what he said,
about his birth, about his life,
about his death.
But facts
are above debate,
which is why the man said,
'One thing I know,
I was blind, but now I see.
. . . Never since the world began
has it been heard that anyone opened the eyes
of a man born blind.'
The fact of an experience
transcends all argument.
I cannot argue with the fact
that today, two thousand years
after Christ walked the streets of Jerusalem,
I can see lives that have been transformed
by their experience of Christ.

Lives filled with love that pours out
for the sick, the hungry and the dying.
People whose response to the love of Christ
is to share that love
in leper colonies and shanty towns;
sane, ordinary people, made extraordinary
by their commitment to the love of Christ.

Lord,
forgive me that so often
I prefer blindness to sight;
that I am afraid of seeing
because seeing
might turn my life upside-down,
alter all my values,
change all my aims and ambitions.
Because, to see through your eyes
changes things;
through your eyes I see
that the only purpose is love,
the only life is love.
In spite of my hesitations,
my reluctance to see the world
through your eyes,
Lord,
heal me, that I may say,
'One thing I know,
I was blind, but now I see.'

OPENING DOORS

'I am the door of the sheep,
through me, anyone who enters shall be saved.'
'. . . I am come that they may have life,
and have it more abundantly.'
                                        – John 10.7, 9, 10

Throughout my life
doors have opened and shut at every stage,
doors into experience,
from home to school,
from work to marriage.
Some doors have swung wide with welcome,
others have remained firmly closed.
And the doors of my mind have opened
from time to time, to thoughts and ideas,
but some doors,
in dimly lit mental passages,
have resisted entry,
refused to open to demands for generosity;
remained shut to requests for forgiveness;
remained barred to appeals for sacrifice.

I wish I had courage enough
to throw open the doors
of my shuttered mind.
So much of my life is locked in.
You, my Lord,
you are the ever open door
that welcomes the sick, the troubled and the outcast.

Within your door lies the abundant life,
for those who dare to accept it.
Doors marked 'Hope', 'Forgiveness'
and 'Peace beyond all understanding'.
Lord, guide my hesitant steps
that I might cross your threshold
and enter into the full life
that is offered to me.

So often
when I am in need of help and support
I seem to run in every direction
except towards you.
I race to hammer against the gnarled and ancient door
marked 'Worldly Widsom',
and in my panic, pass your door
and fail to hear your invitation,
'Come to me, all you who are heavy laden
and I will give you rest.'
Lord, this day,
guide my feet along the path
that leads to you,
that I might enter your door
and find the life you offer
in all its abundance.

SHEEP AND SHEPHERD

'I am the Good Shepherd, I know my sheep
and my sheep know me. The Good Shepherd
lays down his life for the sake of the sheep.'

– John 10.11

Again and again
I am offered the strength and support
of love that will not fail.
And the words of the shepherd
recall the ancient psalm,
'Even though I walk through the valley
of the shadow of death,
I will fear no evil,
for thou art with me.'
With such a shepherd
I should not want,
and yet, time after time,
I find myself distanced from the care and protection
of the shepherd.
Like a startled and terrified lamb
who leaps blindly into ditches and gullies,
I find myself not knowing where to run for safety;
so fraught that even hearing and knowing
the shepherd's voice
I am too confused to know which way to turn.
Sometimes it's hard to imagine
that I am known to God,
that the Good Shepherd knows my name and, more,
sees my distress, knows my doubts,

hears my questions;
but sparrows fall
and my heavenly Father knows.
The hairs on my head are numbered,
and the Shepherd does know me,
better than I know myself.

Heavenly Father, Good Shepherd,
when the events of my life
worry, disturb or even frighten me,
when anxiety makes it difficult
to think straight,
let me hear your voice.
Lead me beside the still waters of your peace.
Remind me that even in the presence
of those I might call enemies
your are with me.
Your strength is available for me.
Good Shepherd,
as I am known to you,
be known to me in goodness and mercy
throughout this day
and all the days of my life.

UNLOCK MY LIFE

'He who keeps his life will die,
he who gives up his life will live.'

— John 12.25

How strange and unacceptable,
the idea of giving up one's life
in order to live.
And yet it is a fact borne out by experience.
The more inward looking I am,
the more I hug my life to myself,
the narrower my life becomes.
And the opposite is equally true.
I can see it in other people who give their lives
unreservedly to others, to a group, to a cause,
their lives seem to open up
and become filled with adventure and experience.
The secret is so simple, I am inclined to overlook it.
We are meant to live
not merely with others, but for others.

Even living alone
it is possible to live for others.
One of the most 'alive' people I ever met
was bed-ridden, paralysed,
but through letters and cards
she reached out with love
to people thousands of miles away.
Without moving from her room
she gave herself to her friends,
and she was alive, full of laughter and news.

And I know it for myself;
I am less anxious, less bored,
there is more laughter, more fun, more 'life'
when I am lost in someone else,
caught up in sharing.
The best way to find life, it seems,
is to lose it in loving someone else.

Lord,
release me,
unlock my life
that I may escape
from the imprisonment of self-centredness
and become truly alive.

IMITATION

'A new commandment I give you,
love one another, as I have loved you.'

– John 13.34

The followers of Christ
are not invited
to embrace a theory
or a principle;
they are given a practical task,
to imitate the love of Christ.
And how did Christ love?
He loved by caring for the sick,
the blind, the paralysed, lepers;
he healed them with love.
He had time for people.
He listened to their questions.
He had time for children.
He not only taught mercy,
but his life was full of compassion
for the poor, for social outcasts,
for known sinners.
So much so
that the self-righteous accused him
of eating and drinking
with prostitutes and collaborators.
'A new commandment I give you,
love one another, as I have loved you.'

His love restored withered limbs and withered lives.
He did not condemn, but helped those who had stumbled
to stand again.

He declared,
'Greater love has no man,
than he lay down his life
for his friends.'
And he laid down his life for love of humanity,
and among his last words was a prayer, not for himself,
but for those who took his life. That is how Christ loves.
And to us he says,
'Love one another, as I have loved you.'

Lord,
May I attempt to imitate you.
May my desire to offer friendship to the friendless
become a fact.
May I not talk of needs
but attempt to meet them.
May I be truly forgiving and compassionate,
in comforting the troubled,
in having time for young and old.
Help me to obey your commandment
that this day I might begin to love
as you have loved me.

THE BEGINNING AND THE END

'I am the way, the truth and the life.'

— John 14.6

If only I knew what to do.
If only I knew how to live.
Each succeeding generation asks,
as I have asked,
'How shall I decide?'
'Where shall I go?'
'Which path will lead to life?'
'How will I know the way?'
And how simple, how straightforward,
is Christ's reply,
'I am the way, the truth and the life'.
And I only have to look at Christ
to know what that means.
It means
the hungry are fed,

the thirsty given drink,
the naked clothed,
the sorrowful comforted.
It means that love
is the beginning and the end
of the road.

How ironic
that Pontius Pilate should ask,
'What is truth?'
when there, in the person of Christ,
truth stared him in the face.
And while we quibble about the virgin birth,
or split hairs about stones being rolled from tombs,
we avoid the truth, which is Christ himself.
The first who is last,
the Son of Man who came, not to be served,
but to serve and to give his life.

43

Who taught,
'Unless you die unto yourself
you will not have life',
'Love one another as I have loved you.'
His love is the truth,
Christ's self-denying love,
that is the truth.

Lord, in you I see
that the way is love,
that truth is love,
and life, real life, is the life of love.
I hesitate to tread in your footsteps
because my courage wavers
on the path of self-denial.
Lord,
though I stumble,
though I fail,
though my imitation of your love is feeble,
though I am easily distracted and tempted
and want to stray down easier paths,
in your mercy, forgive me.
In spite of my faint-heartedness
guide me in the way,
and support me with your truth
that I might find life in you
who are the way, the truth and the life.

MEDITATIONS ON THE
LETTER OF ST PAUL
TO THE ROMANS

TO PRAY UNSELFISHLY

Who do I 'mention always' in my prayers?
If I am honest, I must admit
that I pray, most often, for myself.
'Dear God, help me',
is my most frequent prayer.
When things go wrong at work,
when I am in difficulty with friends,
when there is trouble in the family,
when decisions must be made,
when I am ill,
if I have a daily prayer,
it lies in those self-centred words,
'help me'.

I wish I could be more generous
in my prayers.
At the very least I should pray
for those who love me.
I wish also that I could pray
for those who have let me down.
I wish I could pray
for those who have hurt me.
I wish I could pray
for those who anger me.
Lord, help me to pray unselfishly.

Lord,
you know my problems
without my listing them.
Let me lay them before you
and trust in your love.
Instead of praying for myself,
may I be quiet in your presence
and let your love enter me,
permeate my brain,
clothe my thoughts,
so that your love may transform
panic into calm,
anger into forgiveness,
bitterness into friendship.
Lord, teach me to pray
not for myself
but for your love.

STANDING FIRM

'For I am not ashamed of the Gospel.'

– Romans 1.16

I am not ashamed,
but I would like the Gospel
to be intellectually respectable,
so I talk about
'a spiritual dimension to life',
rather than declare faith in a living God.
I am not ashamed of the Gospel,
but I talk about
'reflecting' or 'thinking deeply',
rather than admit to saying my prayers.
I am not ashamed of the Gospel,
but I talk about
'a continuing form of existence',
rather than confess my belief
in resurrection from the dead.

I am not ashamed of the Gospel,
but I am afraid
of what people might think of me.
I don't want them to say
that I'm a 'Holy Joe',
nor think of me
as a 'religious nut', a crank,
so I don't talk about my deepest thoughts,
it is too embarrassing.
It's not that I'm ashamed, but
badinage is more comfortable
than attempting to share the faith
that gives meaning to my life.

Lord, enable me,
in your strength,
to stand firm in the faith,
to hear jokes and cynicism
with humour and patience,
but let me never deny you
by silence.
In the face of malicious gossip
or deceit or obscenity,
let me see everything,
speak everything,
as in your presence.
Save me from sanctimonious humbug,
prevent me from pious fraud,
but let me be loyal.
Let me not be ashamed of the Gospel,
but rather let me dare
to delight in its truth.

BACKBONE

'Since we are justified by faith
we have peace with God
through our Lord Jesus Christ.
. . . more than that,
we rejoice in our sufferings,
knowing that suffering produces endurance,
and endurance produces character,
and character produces hope,
and hope does not disappoint us,
because God's love
has poured into our hearts
through the Holy Spirit . . .'

— Romans 5.1-5

I can accept
that suffering produces endurance
and in endurance hope is born,
but what hope can enable me
to rejoice in suffering?
Unless it is the hope
that ultimately God's love
defeats all suffering,
defeats pain and anxiety,
defeats even death.

Lord, give me the knowledge
of your conquering love,
that no matter what I may suffer
I may know your peace.

May the hope of Christ
grow in me.
May the passion of Christ
be the source of my endurance.
May the love of Christ
be my backbone.
May the peace of Christ
steady my feet.
May the promises of Christ
support me.
And may every closing of my eyes
be in faith
that my every rising
is in him. Amen.

DYING TO MYSELF

'Why, one will hardly die
for a righteous man –
though perhaps for a good man
one will dare to die.
But God shows his love for us
in that while we were yet sinners
Christ died for us.'

– Romans 5.7-8

Lord,
you once said
'Anyone can love his friends,
but I say to you,
love your enemies.'
And you demonstrated that love
by dying for your enemies.
The amazing fact,
so hard to accept,
is that God
is for the godless and the godly.
His love is for those who love him
and those who do *not* love him.

I have yet to learn
how to give my life
for those I love.
Such total commitment
I have offered in words,
but in fact
I only give part of myself,
part of my time,
part of my life.

Within me
is a great desire
to keep my life for myself,
and to share it sparingly.
The wild abandon and vigour
of your giving
seems far beyond me.
The brightness of your love
reveals how pale and timid
is my love.

Lord,
you said, 'Unless you die to yourself,
you shall not live.'
If real life is only to be found
by dying to myself,
help me to turn my eyes
away from selfish preoccupation
to find life
in those I have been given to love,
not only my family
but everyone, from neighbours
to people dying of hunger
in distant lands.
Lord,
as you gave your life for me,
help me to offer my life for you.

DELIVER ME

'I do not understand my own actions.
For I do not do what I want,
but I do the very thing I hate.
I do not do the good I want,
but the evil I do not want
is what I do.'

— Romans 7.15, 19

How many times have I fumed
at the person I wanted to embrace?
How many times have I walked away
when everything within me
has shouted, 'Stay'?
What emotion, pride or sheer perversity
makes me do the opposite
of what I really want?

There seems to be a flaw
in human nature,
a leaning towards the wicked;
or why else do we favour bad news?
Why are we fascinated
by slanging matches, trickery
and even violence,
when we have the choice
of being soothed by gentleness,
warmed by kindness,
charmed by love?
Why do I listen to,
why do I watch,
why do I do
the very thing I hate?

'Wretched man that I am!
Who will deliver me . . .?
Jesus Christ our Lord,
thanks be to God!'

Lord,
you are the love
that outlives all hatred.
You are the peace
that no anger can destroy.
You are the life
that defeats the death
that lurks in every sin.
You are the way, the truth and the life.
Wretched man that I am,
from all my failings,
Lord, deliver me.

THIS CHILD OF GOD

'When we cry, "Abba! Father!"
it is the Spirit himself
bearing witness with our spirit
that we are children of God,
. . . and fellow heirs with Christ,
provided we suffer with him
that we may also be glorified with him.'

– Romans 8.15-17

Jesus taught us to say,
'Our Father'
and when we cry, 'Father',
even in desperation,
in some mysterious way
the Holy Spirit, the Spirit of Christ,
enters that cry,
and the Father, hearing the voices
of lost children, prodigals,
turns and comes to meet us.

The children of God
are not immune to suffering,
but neither was Christ.
Nor is it a light thing
to be a child of God,
a fellow heir with Christ.
A share in your glory, Lord,
seems to mean a share in your suffering.
If this is true,
put your spirit in me,
so that like you, and with you,
I might see my suffering transformed
from master to servant.

To be a child of God
opens up a world
where the things of the spirit
have more reality
than earthly treasures,
where suffering is vanquished
and love reigns.
I confess,
that though I try to reach out
to the kingdom of the spirit,
this child of God
still has one foot firmly placed
in the world of material things.
Like the Prodigal,
lost in a far off land,
I am calling;
Father, forgive me
and come to me.

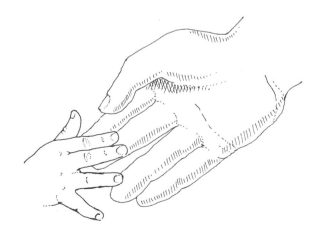

TOO DEEP FOR WORDS

'We do not know even
how to pray as we should,
but the Holy Spirit intercedes for us
with groans too deep for words.'

— Romans 8.26

How often, in prayer,
have I struggled
to find the right words.
How often have I fought
a losing battle
with wandering thoughts,
lost and distracted
in a maze of anxiety.
How often have I felt
that my prayers were inadequate,
feeble, wretched and impoverished;
when the only word I needed
was, 'Father'.

In prayer
I have no need to explain,
no need to persuade or convince,
for the Father knows more about me
than I know myself;
knows the stresses
that I have absorbed unconsciously,
knows my weaknesses, my motives.
There is no formula of words
to gain a right access to God.

If I do not understand myself
then how much beyond my comprehension
is the wisdom of God?
All I need to do
is to dare to come into his presence
with the single word, 'Father'.

Father,
in your presence
I am in prayer,
I want to pray according to your will,
but my own will,
my own desires
imprison my prayers.
Father,
let me not deafen your voice
with my incoherent babble.
Let me be silent in your presence.
Let me trust your Holy Spirit
to speak for me and through me,
with sighs too deep for words.
Let it be enough for me to say,
'Father'.

WHO IS AGAINST US?

'If God is for us,
who is against us?'

— Romans 8.31

It is easier to believe
that God is for us
on a sunny day, a holiday
when family and friends
surround us.
But alone,
with winter's rain on the windows,
when nothing is going right,
then it is hard to accept the idea
that God is for us.
Yet it was in the bleakness
of a crucifixion
that God revealed the love
that remains constant,
even in the darkest hour.

Men and women
have faced persecution and imprisonment;
have resisted the torments of wickedness
strengthened only by faith
in the promise that God is with us
to the end of time.
Illness and calamity of every description
have been endured in the knowledge
that God is for us.

If the gates of hell
cannot prevail against his word
then no trial that I face,
no pain, no problem,
can ever defeat the love of God.

Lord,
in the difficulties that surround me,
in the decisions I have to face,
in the struggle to survive
in what sometimes seems
a hostile world,
may I have faith enough
to declare with confidence
'If God is for us,
who is against us?'.

'For I am convinced
that neither death, nor life,
nor angels, nor principalities,
nor things present, nor things to come,
nor height, nor depth,
no, nothing – in all creation,
can separate us
from the love of God
in Christ Jesus our Lord.'

SEEING MYSELF

'. . . I bid everyone among you
not to think of himself more highly
than he ought to think,
but to think with sober judgement . . .'

– Romans 12.3

It is difficult to see myself
as I really am,
to make a true assessment.
It's not that I think more highly
of myself than I should,
but I am inclined
to remember my strengths
rather than my weaknesses.
Rows and arguments begin
when we refuse to consider
the possibility of being wrong,
and I am no exception.

In the photographs and snapshots
in the family album
I am nearly always smiling.
I compose my face for the camera
so that the only pictures I see of myself
are of me on my best behaviour.
A true assessment of myself,
a true picture, would mean
seeing my face in heated debate,
seeing the cynicism, the anger, the hardness.
More, it would mean seeing inside my mind,
as perhaps only God sees.

Lord,
help me to see myself
through your eyes;
to see the pride
that makes me say and do
the things that hurt;
to see the selfishness
that makes me insist
on my own way;
to see the meanness
that checks me, prevents me
from sharing, giving, loving.
Help me to see the qualities
of those around me;
that in seeing,
generosity of heart and mind
might be born anew
in me.

ARMOUR OF LIGHT

'Do not be overcome by evil,
but overcome evil with good.'

– Romans 12.21

The natural response to evil
seems to be a desire
to strike back in like manner,
blow for blow,
to return insult for insult.
How often have I thought.
'I'll teach him, I'll show him,
I'll get him for that.'
Thoughts of revenge
feed the evil within,
churn the mind,
gnaw the temper,
and well-fed on anger,
evil grows stronger.

Evil thrives on evil,
wickedness does not destroy wickedness
but multiplies it.
Darkness added to darkness
does not bring light,
it only makes the darkness more intense.
Revenge, tit-for-tat,
a grudge held and brooded on,
does not defeat the original wrong
but increases it.
Only goodness diminishes evil.
Only light disperses the darkness.

The evil that destroys inner peace
seeks out the shadowy corners
of my mind,
and creeps in
where thoughts are darkest,
for evil does not like the light.

Lord,
let me put on the armour of light
that evil may not penetrate.
Let me put on Jesus Christ
like a protective mantle
that I may overcome evil
with his goodness.
May what is good in me
reveal the light of Christ,
and in that light
may I know his peace. Amen.

INDEX OF FIRST LINES